NIGERIA

MAJOR WORLD NATIONS
NIGERIA

Nicholas Freville

CHELSEA HOUSE PUBLISHERS
Philadelphia

Chelsea House Publishers

Copyright © 2000 by Chelsea House Publishers,
a division of Main Line Book Co.
All rights reserved.
Printed in Malaysia

First Printing.

1 3 5 7 9 8 6 4 2

Library of Congress Cataloging-in-Publication Data

Freville, Nicholas.
Nigeria / Nicholas Freville.
p.   cm. — (Major world nations)
Summary: An overview of the history, geography, economy,
government, people, and culture of the African nation of Nigeria.
ISBN 0-7910-5390-3
1. Nigeria—Juvenile literature. [1. Nigeria.] I. Title. II. Series.
DT515.22 .F74   1999
966.9—dc21   99-13782
CIP

ACKNOWLEDGEMENTS

The Author and Publishers are grateful to the following organizations and individuals
for permission to reproduce copyright photographs in this book:
Colorpix; The Commonwealth Institute; Keystone Press Agency; The Nigerian
High Commission; Shell Photographic Services; Spectrum Colour Library;
and The United Africa Company.

CONTENTS

FACTS AT A GLANCE

Land and People

Official Name	Federal Republic of Nigeria
Location	West Africa
Area	356,669 square miles (923, 768 square kilometers)
Climate	Equatorial in the south; tropical in the central area; hot and very dry in the north
Capital	Abuja
Other Cities	Lagos, Ibadan, Kano, Ogbomosho, Benin City, Port Harcourt
Population	110,500,000
Population Distribution	Urban, 40.1 percent; rural, 59.9 percent
Major Rivers	Niger, Benue
Highest Point	Chapal Waddi (2,419 meters)
Official Language	English
Other Languages	Over 250 tribal languages
Ethnic Groups	Over 250 ethnic tribes—the four largest are the Yoruba, the Hausa, the Fulani, and the Igbo

Religions	Muslim, 50 percent; Christian, 40 percent; indigenous beliefs, 10 percent
Literacy Rate	57 percent
Average Life Expectancy	Males, 53.5 years; females, 55.9 years

Economy

Natural Resources	Palm oil, rubber, oil, columbite
Division of Labor Force	Agriculture, 54 percent; industry and services, 19 percent; government, 15 percent
Agricultural Products	Peanuts, cotton, palm oil, cocoa, rice, yams, livestock
Other Products	Rubber, hides and skins
Industries	Crude oil, coal, textiles, fertilizers, tin
Major Imports	Machinery and transportation equipment, food, manufactured good
Major Exports	Cocoa, rubber, petroleum and petroleum products
Major Trading Partners	United States, European Union, Japan
Currency	Naira

Government

Form of Government	Military regime
Government Bodies	National Assembly
Formal Head of State	Chairman of the Provisional Ruling Council

HISTORY AT A GLANCE

2nd-18th centuries   The Hausa tribe forms city-states in the north of the area now called Nigeria. Many different tribes inhabit western Africa. Each has different customs and beliefs. Some are warriors, some are farmers, some are hunters.

13th century   Muslims come into the area spreading the teachings of the Islam religion throughout West Africa.

late 15th century   The Portuguese explorers reach Africa and start trading in ivory and pepper (spices were a precious commodity in those days).

15th-17th centuries   The city of Lagos becomes one of the main centers of the slave trade. Some powerful African chiefs capture the weaker tribes and sell them to the slave traders.

1795   A Scottish explorer, Mungo Park, is the first European to find the great Niger River and the rich lands surrounding it.

1807   Britain, now considering the land of Nigeria as part of its commonwealth, outlaws slavery and slave trade. The British go on to exploit the Nigerian tribespeople, taking over their natural resources, changing their farms from food producing enterprises to export-producing enterprises, forcing them to work for them for extremely low wages. Malnutrition among the native population soon follows.

1860s The Royal Niger Company, the largest of all the trading companies operating in Africa, is given the right by the British to make treaties with the chiefs of the tribes on the Guinea coast and to set up courts of law.

early 20th century The British government sends aid to its people trading in Africa. One of the men sent, F. D. Lugard, unites the region under the Crown Colony of Nigeria. The colony is divided into three regions–Northern, Western, and Eastern. Its capital is created in Lagos.

1950s Nigerians begin the process of becoming an independent country from Great Britain.

1960 Nigeria becomes an independent country and a new constitution is approved.

1963 Nigeria officially declares itself the Federal Republic of Nigeria. Nnamdi Azikiwe ("Zik") becomes the first president of the republic. Nigeria becomes a member of the Organization of African States, a group formed so African countries could work together to make a better life for all Africans.

1963-1973 Factories, banks, and transportation companies are set up. Oil and coal are discovered near the coast in the Eastern region. Nigeria is lent money by foreign countries in an attempt to help the growing republic. There is a period of an oil boom with Nigeria's production of oil greatly increasing, bringing new wealth to the country.

1966   In January, because of widespread financial corruption in the government it is overthrown, and General Ironsi, a member of the Igbo tribe, becomes the leader of Nigeria. In July, Ironsi is murdered because of the jealousy and rivalry between the tribes that would plague Nigeria for many decades.

1967   The Igbo tribe decides to make the Eastern Region an independent country and they call it the Republic of Biafra. A war for independence breaks out between Nigeria and this break-away state.

1970   After a long, hard war in which nearly one million people die from the fighting and starvation, Biafra surrenders and again becomes part of Nigeria.

1979   The military leaders who took over the Nigerian government proclaim a new democratic constitution.

1980s Abuja, a new capital city, is planned and built in the central area of Nigeria.

1983   A military coup takes over the government once again after the failure of democracy and much economic turmoil.

1985   Still another military coup takes place, Nigeria's sixth such coup in 20 years. The leader, Major General Ibrahim Babangida, tries to make economic reforms, and promises to allow for civilian rule by the early 1990s.

1991 The federal government is officially moved to the new capital city of Abuja.

1993 Babangida establishes a transitional government. The first elections are held but they end in chaos and another military coup takes place stopping any transition to democracy.

1997 The first step is taken to again try to return to civilian rule with the registration of voters. The transition again is not without its problems and when local elections are held, with an amazing 90 percent participation, some violence and protest occurs.

1

The Birth of Nigeria

Had I asked my great-grandfather to tell me something about a place called Nigeria in tropical Africa, he would have informed me that there was no such country.

To be sure, he might have known the name Niger; it was the name of a huge river, the longest in West Africa. Many people had heard the name, but very few knew exactly where the river was. A traveling Arab from Tangier had first written about the Niger many hundreds of years ago. As a result, mapmakers started decorating their maps of Africa with a new river; on some maps it flowed westward, on some to the east, on some it got lost in the sands of the Sahara.

In the meantime, the merchants and traders of the Mediterranean lands bought shipments of ivory and gold, ebony and other valuable timber, carvings and leather goods. Slowly the news spread that most of these goods came from the land of the big river which ran through the desert. Then it was only a question of time until somebody from the Western world "discovered" this fabled country.

A young Scotsman named Mungo Park was the first European to find the river that was to give its name to the country. He was the first to find that the river flowed across from west to east and then down to the south. He must have been a young man of great

It must have been a scene very similar to this that met the eye of the first trader who ventured up-river from the coast.

courage, for he went there twice, in 1795 and 1805. In the end he died, with all the members of his expedition, in one of the river's swollen rapids.

Mungo Park, and the other explorers who followed him to Africa, came from the west or the north. But for many years previously seafarers had visited the Gulf of Guinea, in the "armpit" of Africa. The sailors came to buy slaves whom they took back to work in the plantations of the New World. Portuguese, Spanish, British, French, and Dutch sailors knew the Guinea coast. In fact, many of the coastal towns—such as Calabar—were given their names by the captains of the old slave ships.

The African coast was as rich as the country which lay beyond it. When slave trading finally came to an end in 1840, as a result of the passing of laws against slavery, trading in goods actually increased. This was partly because a British squadron had been sent to keep the peace in the coastal region known as the Bight of Biafra. What could be more natural than for the traders to sail up the broad river estuaries and follow the course of the rivers as far as they were navigable?

By the 1860s, many individual traders and companies were competing for trade along the Guinea coast, and making treaties with the neighboring chiefs. Gradually, one trading company became stronger and more active than all the others. This company was given a royal charter and became known as the Royal Niger Company.

The royal charter was a very important document. It gave the company the right to make treaties with the chiefs, to establish its own police force and to set up courts of law—in other words, to govern the country.

At the end of the 19th century, quite a lot was known about the huge river called Niger. The powerful trading company of the same name was well established along the coast to the east and west of the swampy estuary and, of course, up the river. But there was still no mention at that time of a country called Nigeria.

The region was inhabited by many different tribes, such as the Igbos, Ibibios, Tivs, and Yorubas. In some of the tribal regions there were highly developed city-states such as Benin and Ife. Further to the north, where the great river turns from the west to the south, there were mighty rulers called emirs. Some of them ruled empires which were at least 1,000 years old. They were war-like and powerful. And, unlike the other Nigerians, they were Muslims. This means that they followed the religion established by Mohammed, the prophet who lived in Arabia in the sixth century A.D. It is thought that the Muslim religion was introduced into this region by Mohammedans in the 13th century.

The Royal Niger Company had dealings with all these people, as did the missionaries, teachers, and prospectors who followed them to Africa. There were arguments and small-scale wars, and the Europeans found that they needed protection and help.

Finally, much against its will, the British government sent aid. It also sent one of its most outstanding men, F. D. Lugard, who in the early years of the 20th century created the Crown Colony of Nigeria, and thus united the whole region.

Previously, the country had consisted of several protectorates, where people were governed by foreign rule but were not given full rights of citizenship of the ruling country. By making one colony, the inhabitants were granted the same rights as British citizens.

Nigeria is a vast region of about 356,000 square miles (over 921,000 square kilometers); in it live well over 88 million people, many of whom are as different from one another as, say, a Russian is from a Scotsman.

The task which faced Lugard was enormous. He made treaties, but he also conquered by force when he had to, especially in the north. Finally, he succeeded in creating order and in providing an efficient administration for running the huge country.

Since there were three main groups of people in Nigeria, the whole area was divided into three regions. The northern half of the country, where the majority of the people live, became the

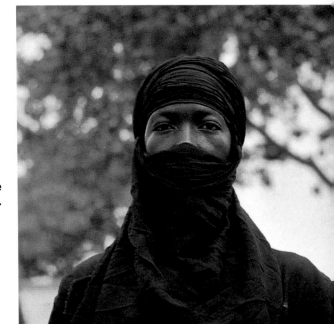

A Hausa from the north of Nigeria.

Northern Region. The southern half was divided into the Western and Eastern Regions.

The Northern Region was inhabited by the Hausa, Fulani, and Kanuri peoples; the Eastern Region by the Igbos; and the Western Region by the Yorubas. Some time ago, another smaller division was created out of the Western Region, called the Midwestern Region, where the Itsekeri people lived, to the west of the Niger River.

Each of the regions originally had an internal government for running its own affairs. But it was found that a national government was needed to look after the affairs of the country as a whole. A state capital was therefore created in Lagos, with regional capitals at Kaduna in the north, Enugu in the east, Benin in the midwest, and Ibadan in the west.

As the British occupied the whole area and treated it as one country, many of the native inhabitants began to think in terms of one country—that is, Nigeria. In addition, they realized that in order to be able to do the same work in their own country as the white man was doing, they would have to have the knowledge and education of the white man; otherwise they could not compete with him. The need for education was made clear, throughout the country, in every way.

Nigerians showed ability and skill in learning, and the colonial government and the voluntary societies did their best to help. The result was that by 1958 there was only one white official to every 20 Nigerians in the whole of the federal administration.

In 1960 Nigeria became a fully independent country, a member

State House. This was the official residence of the Head of State in Lagos when Lagos was the capital.

of the Commonwealth of Nations in its own right, and in 1963 the country was proclaimed the Federal Republic of Nigeria. Let us have a look at independent Nigeria, and at the people who have made it one of the most important and progressive countries in modern Africa.

2

The Making of a Nation

About 60 years ago there was a young Igbo boy from Eastern
Nigeria who was exceptionally intelligent and energetic. As he
grew older, he began to travel, he wrote books and articles and,
in due course, his name became known. People started inquiring
about him. They wanted to know what he thought, and what he
advised them to do. In this way, he acquired a large following, not
only in his own tribe, but all over the country. His name is
Nnamdi Azikiwe, but everybody knows him as "Zik." He became
the owner of newspapers, a writer, a banker and, finally, a political leader. He formed his own political party and he called it
"The National Council of Nigeria and the Cameroons."

Not unnaturally, the people of the Western and Northern
Regions also wished for political representation; so the Yorubas of
the Western Region, under the Yoruba chief Awolowo, formed a
political party called "Action Group"; and the people from the

The man in the white robes is Nnamdi Azikiwe ("Zik"), the first president of Nigeria.

north, headed by the wealthy and influential Sardauna of Sokoto, established their own party and named it "The Northern People's Congress."

These parties all had one thing in common—they taught people to think of themselves as Nigerians, and they all had Nigerian leaders. All three parties were organized in accordance with the laws of the colony and with the help and advice of the British.

21

After much argument, the three parties agreed on the new constitution of their country and when, in 1960, the former colony became independent, everything was ready. "Zik" became governor general and, in 1963, the first president of the republic. Since the president came from the Igbo people in the Eastern Region, Sir Abubakar Tafawa Balewa, a Northerner, was made prime minister. He was very much respected, not only in Africa, but all over the world. Chief Awolowo was also given an important post as he was the representative of the Yorubas from the Western Region. In this way, all three main regions were represented in the new administration.

Independence was celebrated with great rejoicing all over Nigeria. Huge bonfires were lit and the feasting, music, and dancing lasted for days. Then the government of the new country settled down to work.

It had much to do. There were new roads, railways, and airfields to build; schools, training centers, colleges, and hospitals to be established; harbors, mines, wells, and mills to be developed.

Meanwhile, factories, banks, and transportation companies were set up. In addition, oil and large quantities of coal were found near the coast in Eastern Nigeria.

Foreign countries—the United States, Britain, Germany and others—freely helped the young country, lending it money for its needs. Because Nigeria was so rich in natural resources, it could sell more than it bought and easily repay these loans.

Unfortunately, however, some Nigerian ministers and officials were not as honest as they should have been. Money which should have gone to the country found its way into private pockets; many officials and their families became very wealthy while the rest of the people remained poor.

In the end, the people became so angry that they decided, with the help of the Nigerian army, to make an end of what they called the "thief-men." In January 1966, they killed and imprisoned many of the leading men and entrusted the government to an Igbo, General Ironsi.

General Ironsi had been trained in England, and he was a very capable officer. As he was an Igbo, he relied mostly on men of his own tribe to help him to create order and govern the country. The result was that the Yorubas from the west and the Muslim Hausas and Fulanis from the Northern Region became jealous. They were afraid of having too many Igbos in the government. In July 1966, they killed Ironsi and started to make life difficult for the Igbos.

There are about 16 million Igbos in Nigeria. They are very dark and stocky in appearance. They are clever, eager to learn, hardworking, and ambitious. Most of them are Christians. They play an important part, not only in Nigeria, but wherever they go in West Africa, as managers and officials, clerks and merchants.

In many places in the Northern Region the mere presence of Igbo clerks or merchants was enough to start riots. A large number of them were killed and many thousands of them left the north and west in order to return to their homeland in the Eastern Region. It is not surprising to learn that they did not feel very friendly toward the other large tribes in Nigeria, after being hunted through the country, and after General Ironsi was killed in July 1966.

The new head of the Nigerian government was a young officer named Yakubu Gowon. He did his best to come to terms with the Igbos, but the Igbos had had enough. They decided that, with their oil and coal and other natural resources, they could be self-supporting. And so they declared themselves independent of the rest of Nigeria in 1967 and named the Eastern Region the Republic of Biafra, under the leadership of the former governor, Colonel Ojukwu. (Biafra was the old name for the Eastern Region used by the local population before the Europeans came, and the part of the Gulf of Guinea near the Eastern Region, was known for hundreds of years as the Bight of Biafra.)

Federal Nigeria could not accept the Igbos's bid for independence, and the Igbos would not accept a federal government over them. So, unfortunately, the two sides began to fight one another. This resulted in a dreadful civil war which lasted a long time, and

Landscape typical of the Eastern Region, the home of the Igbo people.

caused many deaths and much hardship. Finally, in 1970, the Biafrans surrendered and their leader went into exile.

Nigeria is now divided into 30 states, each with its own parliament. Like the federal parliament and the president of the republic, state parliaments should be democratically elected every four years. However, the country has again come under military rule. Democratic elections were held in 1983, but soon afterward the government was forcibly replaced by a council of army, navy, and air force officers. Since 1983 there has been one military regime after another. In October 1995 the military government promised it would allow a democratic election by October of 1998–a promise Nigerians have heard before.

The chief opponents of the Igbos are the people of what was the Northern Region. There are some 28 million of them and they are mostly Muslims. When Lord Lugard first came to Africa, these people were ruled by their emirs. They had a long history and tradition of which they were very proud. They knew quite a lot about the world in general. Many of them had traveled to Mecca—the holy city to which all Muslims like to make a pilgrimage—and they had traded for many generations with Spain, Italy, Egypt, and the North African coast across the Sahara. They dealt in ivory, timber, and gold; but their main trade was in slaves.

These northern people have a background and social system which is quite different from that of the southerners. They read and speak a form of Arabic. They breed cattle and horses. In ear-

A northern chief with his retainers. The picture shows the difference between these northerners and the rest of the Nigerian people.

lier times, when they dealt in slaves, they always used to regard any kind of ordinary work as something fit only for slaves or Africans from the south. Their rulers were enormously wealthy and had unlimited power. It is not difficult to understand why they became angry when men from the southern tribes came to their land and started telling them what to do and how to do it.

3

The Tribes of Nigeria

Many Nigerians live in the towns and work in offices and factories, but most of them live in the country. They like to stay near their own tribe and very many of them are small farmers.

There are so many different tribes in Nigeria that the Nigerian radio broadcasts in 15 different languages. Some of the bigger tribes are so large that we should call them nations—like the Yorubas, for instance.

All the tribes have their own customs and dances, their chiefs

A baby being carried in his mother's *oja*.

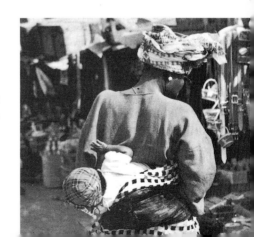

and their societies. They have their own gods, and many of them are not Christians.

Yorubas are friendly and they are very attractive to look at. The men like to dress in a pale blue *agbada*, a long, loose-fitting garment. It is usually embroidered and reaches below the knee. It has an open neck and the wide sleeves can be turned back to the shoulders. The women wear a short blouse and a length of cloth wrapped around them to make a skirt. Over this, around the waist, goes a long, wide piece of cloth called an *oja*. Mothers often carry their babies in the folds of this cloth. Often one can see a mother shopping or working with her baby happily asleep on her back in the oja.

Yoruba women also wear a turban which is tied in a certain way so that the ends stand up above the head. These turbans are very colorful. One can recognize a Yoruba woman a long way away by the shape of her turban or *gele*.

Yoruba men are tall and slim. Many of the best athletes in Nigeria come from the Yoruba nation. They also make good soldiers.

Yorubas believe that their ancestors came many hundreds of years ago from Egypt. They are very proud of their long history.

Scientists and historians say that many of the Yoruba carvings and sculptures look like ancient Egyptian carvings. They also think that their method of using bronze in their works of art is the same as that used by the Egyptians, so it is possible that the legend is true.

The members of the various Yoruba clans have always lived in a very organized manner. They settled in districts, centered

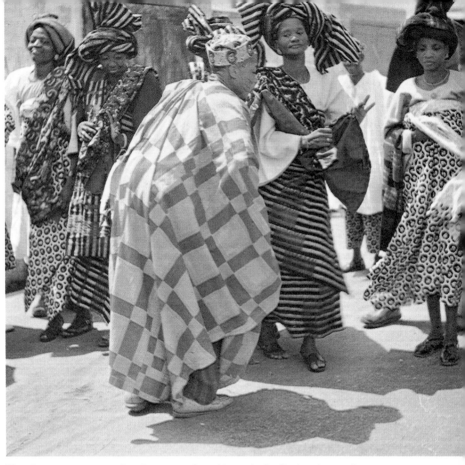

Yoruba women on a festive occasion. Note their distinctive turbans.

around a town where the king lived. The king, or chief, was known as the *Oba,* and he ruled his people from his town residence. He had his counselors, his army, his priests, and other officials. Some, like the kings of Ife, Benin, and Oyo, became very powerful rulers because their countries were so well organized.

29

The people in the country districts live in square, one-room houses built of mud bricks. The floor is beaten earth and there is one window and a door. The doorstep is raised quite high above the ground, so that small babies cannot get out and snakes cannot slide in under the door. In the middle of the room is a stone hearth where the fire is lit for cooking. There is very little furniture—a low stool or two and a hard bed made of bamboo.

Traveling eastward and crossing the Niger by the main bridge near Onitsha, one enters the part of Nigeria where most of the inhabitants belong to the Igbo nation. There are other, smaller tribes called the Ibibio, the Tiv, and the Efik, who live near the coast.

The Igbos have never had kings or powerful chiefs. Each family likes to live alone, and the Igbo villages are also independent of each other.

Igbo people have a great liking for learning. If a student cannot win a scholarship, everybody in the family will work and provide money for his studies. Many Igbo students have gone to universities abroad, their studies paid for by a whole village or a large family.

Whatever an Igbo does, he does well. They are great traders and nothing is too much trouble for them. They live simply, and they make good farmers and careful officials.

Most Igbos are Christian. Those who have studied at the universities return as teachers, doctors, priests, or lawyers and go to the towns to work.

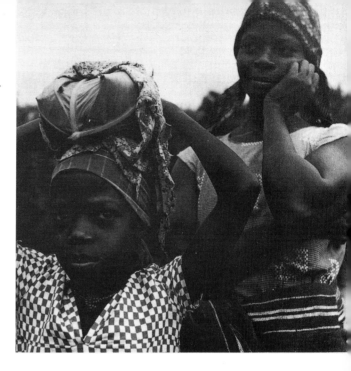

Young Igbo girls.

Both men and women wear an ankle-length "skirt" which is made by wrapping a long piece of cloth around themselves several times and tying the end in a knot. The cloth is very often dark red in color and is decorated with different patterns. The knot can be undone and the last round of the "skirt" pulled up to cover the shoulders.

Women and girls wear headscarves. These are always brightly colored, but much simpler than the Yoruba turbans.

The Igbo farmer builds himself a very simple house. As this area has more rain than other parts of Nigeria, he does not use nails or wire because these would rust away. Instead, he makes a frame of wood and the wooden posts are woven together with creepers which he can find in the forest. When this "basket-house" is ready, he plasters it with clay and covers the roof with banana leaves.

The Igbo houses are small and square and are very easy to repair. They have no windows, just a door. When the farmer makes more money, he builds a stronger house and uses corrugated iron for roofing.

In the north of Nigeria live the Hausas and the Fulanis and, in the northeastern corner, the Kanuris. As we have already seen, all these tribes have been converted to the Muslim religion.

In the past the Hausas were a fierce and warlike nation. They lived under the rule of the emirs, whose word was law. The men were mainly occupied in fighting, raiding, and trading. All the everyday work was done by the women and the slaves.

The Hausa people are not quite as dark as the people living in the southern half of Nigeria. The men dress in long white flowing robes and wear a white turban. Sometimes they wear a dark embroidered cloak over their white robes. The women prefer dark blue or black robes. They wear a covering on the head which can be pulled over to hide the face. Muslim women do not like their faces to be seen by strangers.

Hausas prefer to live in towns. Many of their towns have some fine old buildings, with walls of decorated clay or plaster and beautifully carved doors.

At home, they like to sit on carpets and cushions or on pieces of sheepskin rather than on chairs or stools.

The Hausas are great traders, and many of them travel not only in Nigeria but all over Africa. They enjoy bargaining and will spend a long time haggling over the price of some article; but once a Hausa merchant agrees to something, he will keep his word.

In the rural areas, a Hausa or Fulani village can easily be recognized because all the houses are round. The walls are built of clay, and the roofs are thatched and rise to a point like a cone. There is one door, which is so small that you have to bend low to get in and out, and no windows. Men and women live in separate houses.

The largest tribe after the Hausas is the Fulani tribe. The Fulanis, like the Hausas, have a long history. A hundred years ago, they had a very famous ruler who decided that all the people as far as the Yoruba country should become Muslim. His name

Fulani herdsmen and their flock.

was Usuman Dan Fodio. He created a powerful kingdom in northern Nigeria and waged war against all non-Muslims in the south.

The Fulani dress is much simpler than that of the Hausas. It is a long, straight robe, often pale yellow or pale blue. The men wear a small skullcap and, on important occasions, an embroidered cloak. The women wear a dark dress and sometimes as many as six or eight large earrings. The men shave their heads, but the women tie their hair into tight braids.

The Fulanis are cattle breeders. In very hot weather the herds-

Fulani cattle being ferried across the Benue River. Note the strange-looking hump and the widespread horns.

men wear sun-helmets. These are made of straw, often edged with leather, and shaped like a basket or an upside-down beehive.

Both the Fulanis and the Hausas love horses and take great care of them. Their saddles and bridles are carefully decorated.

The Kanuri is a much smaller tribe. They live in the northeastern part of Nigeria, called Borno. The Kanuris, like the Fulanis, are cattle breeders and they are skillful herdsmen. Their main market town is Maiduguri where they sell their animals as well as many thousands of hides. The cattle have huge horns set wide apart, and they have a hump where the neck and the back meet. Most of the cattle are red-brown, but there is also a bigger, gray-colored breed.

In northeastern Nigeria there is a small tribe—related to the Fulani—which does not live in any one spot. These are the Mbororos, who move about from place to place, stopping wherever there is enough grass for their cattle to graze on. They wander from Lake Chad in the northeast right down to the south. Their herdsmen use small bows and very dangerous arrows, but they are friendly and kind to other travelers.

There is one other group of people in Nigeria which is not called by the name of a tribe but by the place where they live. These are the "creek people" who live near the sea in the river estuaries, swamps, lagoons, and other waterways. They are excellent boatmen and fishermen. The children can swim before they can walk.

The houses of the creek people are built on stilts, right on the

Boats moored on the bank of a creek village.

waterline, so they can step straight into their boats and go fishing. The houses are built of mangrove wood, which does not rot in water. The boats used to be made of the trunks of huge trees, and the first traders and explorers traveled in these, rowed by eight or more oarsmen with short paddles.

4

Rivers Between the Sands and the Sea

If you look at the small inset map in the front of this book showing the whole of Africa, you will see that Nigeria lies south of the Sahara, between the Sahara and the sea.

Two major rivers flow through Nigeria—the Niger, from the west, and the Benue, from the east. The two rivers meet in the middle of the country and turn south, forming a giant Y.

East and west of the trunk of the giant Y, the country is relatively flat; further north, where the rivers separate, the country becomes steeper and more hilly. In this area, which is called the Bauchi highlands or plateau, there are mountains of over 4,000 feet (1,200 meters).

Nigeria is very near the equator, and this means that there is no winter or summer. Instead, there is a rainy season, which starts in May and lasts until October, and a dry season. In the far north near the Sahara there is little rain. The nearer we go towards the sea, the heavier the rainfall.

The temperature in the southern part of Nigeria is always about 80 degrees Fahrenheit (27 degrees Celsius), but the air is very humid and people soon feel tired. In the northern part it can be as hot as 110 degrees Fahrenheit (43 degrees Celsius) and as cool as 67 degrees Fahrenheit (19 degrees Celsius), but it is dry and one can sleep well at night.

Most vegetation grows best in a climate which is hot and wet, and this applies equally in Nigeria. In the southern part of the country there are huge forests extending inland for great distances. Further to the north, the forests become thinner and the country has the appearance of an enormous park. Still further north, where the climate is hot and dry, fewer trees are seen; and as one approaches the Sahara there are more and more bushes and shrubs growing in coarse grass, and fewer trees; this kind of land is called *savannah*. North of the savannah country, the only vegetation is rough grass, and beyond that lies the desert.

The Niger and the Benue, and the Cross River in the extreme southeast, bring water to many parts of Nigeria. By the end of the rainy season, however, these rivers are flooding. Often bridges are washed away and the flood waters tear out huge chunks of earth. Heavy trees float in the rivers and are a danger to steamers or boats. So much water comes down that when the river reaches the flat land near the sea, one riverbed

Landscape typical of northern Nigeria.

is not enough. The flood waters spread over the surrounding countryside and create new channels. That is why the Niger has 13 mouths opening into the sea and the Cross River is simply lost among its many outlets.

The land surrounding these estuaries is swampy and is crisscrossed by waterways and channels, known as creeks. The banks of the creeks are lined with mangrove trees. Each tree forms hundreds of thick, twisted roots above the water, and

A mangrove swamp. The thick, twisted roots of the mangrove trees can be seen on the right of the picture.

these roots go far down into the wet ground. They grow so thickly that it is very hard to cut a way through them.

Where the swamp ends, the forest begins. Some of the trees— such as the iroko, sapele, and obeche—provide very valuable timber, which is used for furniture-making. Bamboo, which is used for many purposes, also grows in profusion. There are creepers and climbing plants hanging everywhere. Tree trunks are covered in shiny green moss. There are palm trees of all sorts, many ferns, and some beautiful orchids. Every now and then one comes across a lovely tree, with clusters of bright red flowers, called Flame-of-the-Forest.

Vegetation grows so quickly in the forests that an unused clearing will be overgrown in a few months' time.

There are not many animals here because there is not enough food for them, but in the morning and evening the air is filled with the noise of millions of crickets. Occasionally one comes across a very small antelope, no bigger than a cat. But most of the animals, chattering little gray monkeys and a variety of birds of the hornbill family, live high up in the tops of trees. There are very few snakes and they are mainly harmless.

Beyond the rain forests, and in northern Nigeria, the inhabitants go hunting. Hunting is done with the help of dogs. These Nigerian hunting dogs cannot bark. They are smooth-haired and are about as big as a terrier. Nigerians call them "pie" dogs. Each one has a little wooden bell around its neck which makes a musical sound. The owner of the dog can recognize the sound of his bell and will know where to go. In many places, especially in the north, many hunters still use spears. Others use muzzle-loading guns with very long barrels, some of which actually have to be held steady by one man while another is firing it.

In the Bauchi highlands there are many baboons. These big monkeys with their doglike faces move about in large troops. Their biggest enemy is not man but the leopard, a beautiful and very dangerous animal which roams around in this region.

Near the Sahara there are antelope and deer. These are always on the move searching for grass to eat and water to drink.

There are snakes in the drier parts of Nigeria. Some are poisonous and dangerous, although they will not attack people

41

unless they are frightened. There are vultures and hyenas, too. Vultures and hyenas are not likable animals, but they do very useful work. When an animal dies in the bush, or a sheep or a goat is lost from the herd, the vultures and hyenas clear away the carcass. Hyenas do not show themselves in daylight, but they will approach a village at night and can be heard howling and "laughing."

5

Lagos and Other Towns

In the middle of the Bight of Benin, in the Gulf of Guinea, a narrow channel from the sea leads into a lagoon. On an island in that lagoon, 500 years ago, Portuguese sailors found a little village; and that is how Lagos—until 1991 the official capital of Nigeria—was discovered.

In those days, the entire area was a giant swamp. Its mosquitoes, damp heat, and tropical diseases gave it the name "white man's grave." But this did not prevent it from becoming one of the main centers of the slave trade, with the powerful African chiefs capturing the weaker tribes and selling them to the slave traders.

In the middle of the 19th century, the British navy was given orders to remove the slavers from the Bight of Benin. In 1861 the powerful king of Lagos agreed to stop raiding for slaves; in return, the British gave him 1,000 bags of cowrie shells, which represented a good deal of wealth. He handed over Lagos to the British, and from that day Lagos began to grow in peace.

Today, Lagos is a thriving and progressive city. There was electric street lighting in Lagos before there was any in London. The roads are paved and there are banks, shops, offices, schools, hospitals, and everything else that a modern city needs.

Lagos has grown so much that the island is not large enough for the nine million inhabitants and it has spilled over onto the mainland. The cities population has increased 20-fold in the last 30 years. At that rate Lagos is expected to be one of the five largest cities in the world by 2025.

One of the many modern buildings in Lagos.

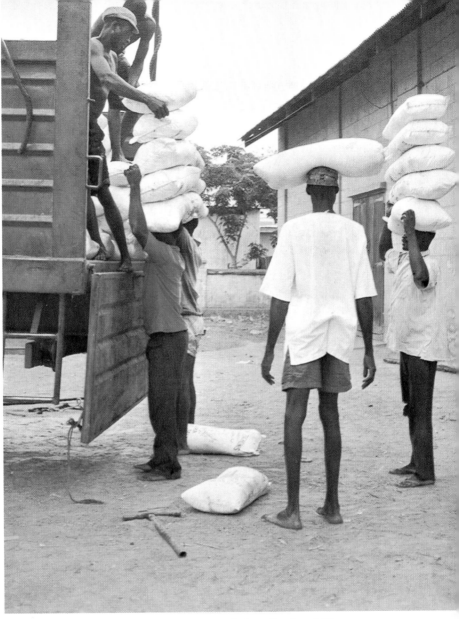

Whatever the burden it is likely to be carried on the head. These men are carrying sacks of salt in Kano.

One of Lagos's main streets has hundreds of small, open-fronted shops, where a great variety of goods are displayed for sale. Nigerians are very fond of colorful clothes, and in these small shops one can find silks, velvets, and cotton materials. Some of these cottons have rather odd designs printed on them—the letters of the alphabet, for instance, or a picture of a telephone. Lagos today is a thriving metropolitan area with expressways connecting its many sections. The main business

A view of Lagos.

district is on the southwestern shore of the island and is considered the heart of the city. Lagos has many industries including metalworks, textiles, automobile assembly, and food processing. Lagos is one of the major seaports of Africa, and the principal port for Nigeria's trade.

It is not a very long train journey from Lagos to the capital of the Oyo State. This is Ibadan, the second largest city in Nigeria with 1,263,000 inhabitants.

Everyone in Nigeria is very proud of Ibadan, which has one of the best universities in Africa. Students come there from all over the English-speaking world. For many years, most of the teachers came from the University of London, but now there are many Nigerian professors lecturing at the place where they were once students themselves.

The university is not very far from the town, which is surrounded by low hills. The buildings are white and airy, and from a distance they look as if they had been cut out with a fretsaw.

Far away, to the north of Nigeria, is the famous city of Kano, the capital of the state of the same name. This ancient city is quite different from the other main towns or cities of Nigeria. The houses are made of dried clay and have flat roofs because there is never much rain. The whole town was originally surrounded by an immense high wall with 13 gates in it but much of the wall is destroyed now. In the midst of the brown houses

A bird's-eye view of the old city of Kano. Its strangely shaped houses are made of dried clay.

rise the two tall, slender turrets of the gleaming white Muslim church—the huge mosque of Kano.

Outside the ancient walled city is the modern town with its factories, shops, and houses. Nearby is Kano Airport, where a trumpeter of the Emir of Kano, sitting on a white racing camel, once used to salute the long-distance jets.

Kano is the town of the Hausas and is one of the biggest towns on the southern edge of the Sahara. It was from here that the caravans set out across the Sahara with slaves, ivory, and gold. Even now there are quite a few camels to be seen.

Because it is on the edge of the desert, there is much dust in this region. For two whole months, the wind blows from the Sahara and the dust makes the air look foggy. This desert wind

48

is called the *harmattan*. When it blows, the men pull the loose fold in their turbans over their faces to protect themselves against the dust.

The capital of the Enugu State is the city of Enugu. It looks very different from Kano, with its wide avenues, squares, and many trees. Coal is mined near the city.

Not far from Enugu is Onitsha, which has a beautiful cathedral and one of the biggest markets in the whole of West Africa.

A federal capital territory was established in 1976 in the cen-

A modern factory in Enugu.

The beautiful gleaming-white mosque of Kano where the inhabitants are followers of the Muslim religion.

tral area of Nigeria. A new capital city was designed and built during the 1980s called Abuja. The site for Abuja was chosen for its central location, its accessibility to the rest of the country, and its room for expansion. The federal government was transferred from Lagos to Abuja in 1991. Abuja has many large government buildings, shops, modern housing, and most of the modern urban amenities. It has its own airport and there are highways connecting Abuja to the other major cities of Nigeria. The University of Abuja was established in 1988.

The cathedral at Onitsha.

There are other important towns in Nigeria, among them Kaduna, the capital of the Kaduna State; Bonny, on the coast; and Port Harcourt, one of the countries largest ports.

6

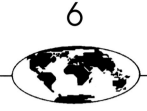

Tribal Chiefs and Customs

Before the Europeans came to Nigeria, the inhabitants lived under the rule of their kings, emirs, and other chiefs. Some of these kings had great power and had many lesser chiefs under them. The Emir of Kano and the Oni of Ife were looked upon as the greatest of rulers.

As we have seen, when Nigeria became independent, it was no longer ruled by tribal chiefs and kings but by a government of ministers. At first this was difficult for many Nigerians to accept. So to make government easier, it was arranged in each region that the ministers should have a council to help them. This council was made up of all the tribal chiefs and was called the House of Chiefs.

The chiefs no longer made the rules and laws, but they advised the government about the laws and customs of their own tribes. The kings and chiefs are held in great respect, even by the members of the government.

The kings of the various tribes of the Yoruba nation all accept the Oba of Ife as the chief king. He is known as the Oni, and he is the keeper of all the sacred objects of the Yorubas. When a new oba, or king, is crowned in one of the smaller Yoruba tribes, he is crowned by the Oni of Ife.

The obas of the Yoruba tribes have their own titles. For example, the Oba of Oyo is called the *Alafin*, the Oba of Abeokuta is the *Alake*, and the Oba of Warri is the *Olu*. These titles all have meanings, such as "the crocodile who devours his enemies," or "the elephant who destroys his opponents." They were invented long ago to frighten enemy tribes.

When one of the obas goes anywhere, it is an occasion for great pomp and display. The oba is dressed in a beautiful embroidered gown and his slippers are decorated with gold and silver. He wears a golden crown and often he carries a long, elaborately decorated staff. His servants bear his sword and stool. Around him are his officials and friends, all dressed in flowing robes. A number of drummers go before him and herald his coming by beating their drums. Immediately behind the oba walks a servant holding a huge umbrella of state over him. This umbrella is colored and decorated and bears the golden badge or crest of the oba—an elephant, perhaps, or a crocodile, or a tortoise.

The obas and the lesser chiefs have many duties to perform. For instance, they are the custodians of the land, which belongs

An Oba, or chief, dressed in ceremonial robes. Note the gold crown and umbrella of state.

to the whole tribe and not to individuals. It is they who make sure that each farmer has a piece of land on which he can raise crops. It is they who give permission for valuable trees to be felled and sold for timber. The chiefs also act as judges for their particular district in the many quarrels and fights which occur in the villages.

The kings and chiefs have their own councils. These are made up of the older men of the tribe. An important chief like the Oni of Ife has his own palace and council chamber. A small tribe can hold a council in the open under the shade of a tree.

The Igbos have no big chiefs. Their place is taken by the elders of the village.

A meeting in progress beneath the shade of a leafy tree.

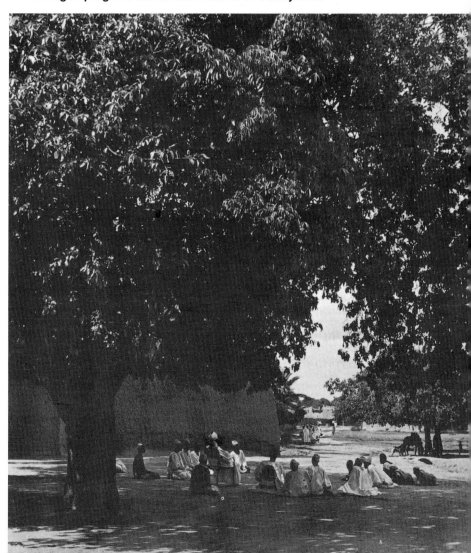

The emirs of northern Nigeria are still much respected. They do not wage war any longer, nor do they make laws, but all their people acknowledge their importance. For many hundreds of years, they have been wealthy and have exercised great authority. Four hundred years ago, when Emir Mousa went on a pilgrimage to Mecca—where the prophet Mohammed was born—it took 1,000 camels to carry his gold.

The emirs held court in their cities. They were surrounded by merchants, travelers, musicians, and many learned men. These learned men were lawyers, doctors, writers, and teachers; they all spoke Arabic and followed the Arab way of life. Each of the emirs had a vast army, chiefly of cavalry, that was armed with swords and spears.

One of the most powerful of emirs was the ruler of Sokoto in northwestern Nigeria. He was so great that he was not called emir, but was given the title of sultan. He was not only a powerful chief, but also the head of all Muslims in Nigeria, and he directed the religious ceremonies.

The present ruler of Sokoto still has a mounted bodyguard and on great occasions hundreds of his people follow him on horseback. When he wishes to entertain his visitors he lines up his horsemen in the distance. Then, at a given signal, they start galloping towards the spectators. In flowing white robes, sabers drawn, lances set, and shouting their war cries, hundreds of horsemen come thundering straight at the visitors. When they are only a short distance away, they suddenly pull up their rearing horses. There is a cloud of dust and a great swirl of horses and men. Then the wonderful display is over. There is no sight like this anywhere else in the world.

When we think of a family, we usually mean a father, mother and children. But in Nigeria, a family means all the people who are related. A Nigerian household will consist of a father and mother and their children, and all the uncles, aunts, cousins, and other relatives who wish to live with them. The head of the household is the man who is able to feed and generally look after this large family. Even a Nigerian who has studied abroad and returns home as a qualified accountant, lawyer, or teacher has to look after all his relatives, not only his own wife and children. He still feels bound by the old tribal customs.

The Emir of Daura (center), one of Nigeria's tribal leaders.

When the Europeans came to Nigeria, they encountered people whom they called witch doctors. In fact, these people were neither witches nor doctors. Some believed in human sacrifice, and did much harm; but many were simply pagan priests. There were others who claimed they could make rain or prevent storms and floods, or that they had the power to foretell the future. All of them knew about medicine. They treated wounds and tried to heal the sick. They learned about the different plants and herbs of the forests and how to use them. There were many illnesses they could cure.

In parts of Nigeria today there are native doctors. They know a great deal about useful plants and herbs. In the Nigerian universities, scientists and doctors are very interested to learn from the native doctors. These people no longer cast bones and sacrifice chickens but try to do their work honestly. Often they advise the sufferer to go to one of the big hospitals to see a qualified doctor.

Perhaps the nicest custom in Nigeria is the hospitality the people offer to strangers. Not only in the towns but also in the poorest village, a stranger will be offered something to eat and drink. The people are friendly, kind, and very interested in anything one tells them. In the villages, a traveler will be given pineapples, bananas, or sugarcane to take on his journey. Nigeria is a very friendly land to travel in.

At one time these people would have gone to the witch doctor for a cure for their sickness. Now more and more people come to hospitals like this one for treatment.

7

Markets

The markets are the shopping centers of Nigeria. The Nigerians love their markets and visit them not only to do their shopping but also to exchange gossip with friends or acquaintances and to hear all the news.

A large, bustling market in the city of Kaduna.

A smaller village market. Nigerians love their markets and come to them not only to buy and sell but also to meet their friends.

In nearly every large village and in all the towns there is a market. A large open space is set aside, and covered stalls are set up all the way around it.

Some markets are very large. One can buy almost anything there: a car or a camera; an electric generator or a top hat. Food, clothes, and cosmetics are all on sale, and the goods come from all over the world—from Africa, America, Europe, and Asia.

People ply their trade in the market—there are mechanics and tailors, and native doctors who sell medicines for various ailments. There are even people who offer their services as letter writers to those who cannot read or write.

You need never go hungry or thirsty on market day. There are snack bars where you can eat fried locusts—or, if you prefer, ice cream—and drink palm wine or beer or tea. And there are jugglers, dancers, and musicians to entertain you.

All the merchants selling the same kind of goods group themselves together. There may be a long row of stalls where shoes are sold. Another section will offer clothing for sale. A very large area will be taken up by sellers of various food. Each seller has a pile of food in front of him—a mound of pineapples, a basketful of mangoes, or a big sackful of maize. Often goods are not sold by weight, but are measured out in cigarette tins, or matchboxes, or cups.

The carpenters, butchers, mechanics, and barbers are men, but nearly all the other stall holders are women. They are very good at their job. Many cannot read or write and they carry all their business in their heads. Some of them are very rich. They live in large houses, have their own servants, and take vacations in Europe. These women have been buying and selling things since they were children. Quite small girls in Nigeria can be seen selling food and fruit. They carry their goods on their heads in a basket or in a big washbasin. By the time they are grown they know everything about the markets.

Buying and selling is done by bargaining. Two people may spend a long time haggling over the price, but once they reach agreement they accept one another's word. If a seller or buyer tried to cheat, he would be beaten and told never to come back.

62

As so many people go to the markets, it is here that important announcements are made—for instance, that children are to be vaccinated in a certain district or that the adult education teacher will visit a village on a certain day.

When Nigerians go to a market they often walk. If the market is a long way away they usually travel by public lorry. These lorries are sometimes very old. They travel all over the country carrying people and their goods. Most of them have a saying painted on them, such as *Better late than never*, or *Trust in God*. When a lorry breaks down or gets stuck in the rainy season, the passengers all get out and help.

8

Transportation

Not many years ago, when somebody had to make a journey to a district where there was no road or railway, he had to walk. Food and other necessities had to be prepared and carefully packed. Then carriers had to be found. Each man carried a load on his head and the procession halted every afternoon, camping out and then packing up and moving on the next morning. Traders, officials, doctors, engineers, and missionaries all traveled in this way. The journeys often took many days and were very expensive.

Nowadays, many stretches of road and railways have been laid, and traveling is no longer the difficult undertaking it once was.

The two most important roads in Nigeria both run from the west to the east. They are part of a network connecting West Africa with East Africa.

The railways were laid in such a way that the two main ports—Lagos and Port Harcourt—are connected with the capital cities of the chief states. The first locomotives used wood for fuel. Later,

A Nigerian water-bus. Where there are few roads and railways, the rivers are often used for getting from place to place.

coal was discovered near Enugu and this was used instead. Since then, oil has been found, and an increasing number of diesel trains have been put into service. Today there is more than 2,200 miles (3,557 kilometers) of track connecting Nigeria's cities.

The waterways, too, are used for trade and travel. Boats can sail right up the Niger River to Jebba, and up the Benue River as far as Yola; and during the rainy season, they can go much further.

But perhaps the most useful form of transportation in Nigeria is the airplane. All the main towns have an airport, and many smaller places have a landing field which can be used by light aircraft. Now an engineer can go and examine a bridge and a doctor can treat a sick person very quickly. Nigerians like flying and they make good pilots.

Modern rail, road, and river transportation has helped the

Nigerians in another way as well. It has made it possible for farmers and producers to work together and sell their produce jointly—that is, to cooperate. Near Kano, thousands of small farmers grow groundnuts on their little plots of land. At harvest time the farmers bring the nuts to the cooperative society, which stores, transports, and sells their produce for them. There are thousands of cooperative societies in Nigeria, all managed by Nigerians.

A very interesting cooperative society was the Community of the Apostles. In 1940, a few fishermen in a poor village in western Nigeria decided that they wanted a better life for their families, so they pooled their resources. Their source of income was fish, which they sold in Lagos. The money was kept by their treasurer and every family was given what it needed. The rest of the money was used to build better houses, schools, hospitals, and nurseries. The poor muddy fishing village became a pleasant, healthy and prosperous town.

As the roads and railways reached out further, it became possible to take better care of the people. Doctors and nurses could travel to out-of-the-way places and explain to people how to avoid diseases. Mosquitoes and certain flies carry diseases like malaria, yellow fever, sleeping sickness, and river-blindness, which make people so weak that they cannot work. Everywhere in Nigeria there are people now whose job it is to destroy these flies and mosquitoes.

9

Food

Nigerian people live very simply. They have one big—sometimes very big—meal in the afternoon, and a small one in the evening before they go to bed. Nearly all their food is homegrown and is prepared at home. Instead of plates or dishes, Nigerians use baskets of plaited straw, and they eat with their fingers.

Some food is quite easy to cultivate. In the wet, warm south they grow root vegetables such as yams, cocoyams, and sweet potatoes. The yam is a tuberous plant like the potato. It has a black outer skin and is white inside. Yams can be boiled or mashed, just like potatoes.

In the drier parts of the country, much maize (corn) is grown. The maize is dried and ground, and the rough flour is made into a dough. This dough, which is called *foo-foo*, can be eaten on its own or with some kind of sauce.

Another popular food is *garri*. This is made from the roots of a shrub called the cassava. The roots are pounded in tall wooden mortars and then boiled or fried.

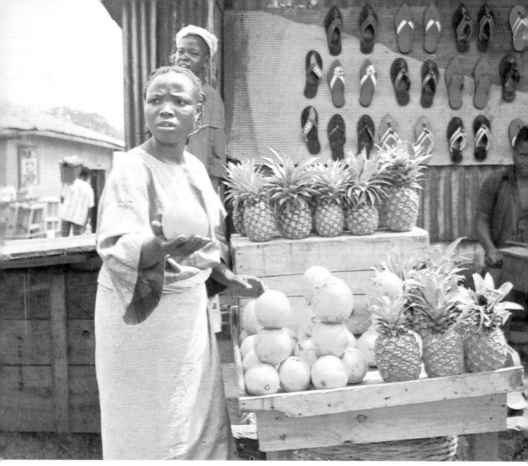

A girl selling fruit in a market in Ibadan.

Nigerians like rice and in the rainy parts of the country rice grows well. There is very little bread, because the climate is not suitable for wheat-growing.

Meat can be obtained in all the markets, but it is expensive, and for this reason the Nigerians keep a lot of hens and ducks.

They also like goat meat and antelope meat, and the meat of

68

hedgehogs and of giant water snakes—both of which taste very good.

In the north, where huge herds of cattle are kept, the Fulani and Kanuri women make butter, but the people do not drink much milk—in fact, most milk is imported in tins.

Much dried fish is brought into Nigeria from Europe. It comes in big bundles looking like dry sticks of wood. Nigerians use this fish for soups or to make sauces for garri, foo-foo, and yams.

Nigeria grows a great deal of fruit of all kinds. Bananas can be seen growing in almost every garden. There are paw-paws, delicious mangoes, and pineapples—which can also be found growing wild in forest clearings. Oranges, limes, and grapefruits grow in many orchards.

A less well-known crop, from which a very well-known drink is made, is the kola nut. The kola trees produce a fruit which looks like a green grapefruit. In due course, the green outer skin falls away, revealing the silver and pink nuts. Cola sodas are made from the juice of these nuts. Africans chew them when they are thirsty. If a Nigerian gives you a kola nut, it is a sign of friendship.

Sugarcane can be bought in the markets, but many people grow it at home. The hard outer casing, which is peeled away, looks like green bamboo. The white inner fibers are juicy and sweet.

For cooking, Nigerians use oil. In the north, groundnut oil is used and in the south, palm oil.

10

Natural Resources

Nigeria grows thousands of tons of groundnuts—which we call peanuts—both for its own use and for sale abroad. The low groundnut plant has a tangle of shoots above the ground, the "nuts," which are actually seeds, forming underground. When they are ripe, the whole family helps to harvest them. The roots are pulled up and the nuts are dried in the sun. The oil which is pressed out of the nut is used for cooking and the rest of the nut is eaten as food.

Another kind of oil comes from the oil palm. When we eat margarine or use soap, it is almost certain that the palm oil which they contain comes from Nigeria. This oil is the chief crop in the Eastern Region of the country.

The oil palm likes a warm, wet climate. The tree grows straight up to a height of over 30 feet (nine meters) or more.

A harvest of groundnuts. The plants have been pulled up, and the "nuts," which grow under the ground, have now been laid out to dry in the sun.

There the leaves branch out. The fruit grows in bunches at the base of the leaves. Thousands of little oil-palm fruits make up one of these bunches, each bunch the size of a large soccer ball.

Each fruit consists of a hard nut covered by a softer shell. The oil which is pressed from the shell is called palm oil, and the oil which is extracted from the nut is known as palm ker-

71

nel oil. After the bunches of fruit have been cut down, they are collected and taken in lorries to the oil mill. On some very big plantations there is a small railway which takes the produce to the mills. The oil mills are like factories and the biggest of them is at Port Harcourt.

In the mills, the single fruits are separated from the stems. Then the soft outer shell is separated from the hard kernel. Big presses squeeze the palm oil out of the shells. The oil is cleaned

Bunches of oil-palm fruits; each little fruit has a soft outer shell and a hard inner nut, and oil is extracted from both shell and nut.

Tapping a rubber tree.

and piped into storage tanks. Later it is piped direct to the docks and into waiting ships.

The palm kernel oil is used to make margarine, and the

crushed and dried kernels are fed to milking cows. Country people in Nigeria have their own use for palm oil. When it starts to rain, instead of putting on a raincoat they take off their clothes. Then they smear their bodies with palm oil and the rain rolls off their oily skin. They say it is much better than having to go about in wet clothes.

Cocoa is grown in the western and midwestern states. It is

A young rubber plantation.

A Nigerian tin mine.

from the cocoa bean that chocolate is made. The cocoa beans grow inside a shell which is a little smaller than a rugby ball.

Cocoa trees are difficult to grow. The seedlings like warmth, but they also like shade, so they are planted under other trees.

75

Much rubber is produced in Nigeria. The rubber trees grow in plantations, many of them covering vast areas. When the rubber is ready to be collected, a length of bark is cut off around the trunk. Then a small cup is fastened to the trunk. Where the bark has been cut the tree "bleeds" and a white liquid called latex drips into the cup. The liquid is collected and smoked, and becomes the raw rubber.

Some of Nigeria's wealth, such as tin, is to be found below the ground. There are important mines in Benue-Plateau State. The miners direct strong jets of water into the hillsides. The earth crumbles and most of it is washed away. The heavy part—which holds the tin—remains and this is transported to the factories.

Nigeria also has columbite, a valuable substance used for making steel extra hard. With columbite better jet engines can be manufactured.

Everyone in Nigeria was glad when coal was discovered near Enugu in the East Central State. Although it is not as hard or as black as the best coal, it is still very useful to the country.

People were even more pleased when, after a long search, oil was found in the swampy eastern coastal area. There is enough oil for the whole of Nigeria, and a surplus besides which is exported to other countries. A large port was built at Bonny near the oilfields. It has a specially long jetty so that ships can come and fill up with oil which is pumped out through pipelines. Now there are four more oil terminals.

A Nigerian member of an oil-drilling crew at work.

As time goes on, more and more oil is being found in Nigeria. The quality of this oil is excellent and it is being exported in large quantities, thus improving the country's economy.

There is one substance, more important than all the others, which has been found under the ground; and that is water. During the dry season many small rivers and streams disappear. Without water, animals die of thirst, and nothing will grow. For many years the governments of Britain and Nigeria employed scientists to search for water. At last the experts dis-

A tanker terminal. The jetty which can be seen in the picture is for the use of small craft only. The one for tankers goes much further out to sea.

This picture of a water pumping-station scheme may appear ordinary but to the people of Nigeria it represents one of the miracles of modern scientific progress.

covered that if they bored a sufficiently deep hole in the earth, they would reach water. These very deep wells are called "artesian wells," and they have saved many lives. There are now thousands of these wells in Nigeria and the government hopes that eventually every small village will have its own supply of water.

11

Education and Art

Nigerian children have to work very hard when they first go to school. At home with their families they speak their own tribal languages. At school, all the classes are held in English, so they have to start learning what for them is a foreign language.

Children at school in northern Nigeria.

Some village schools are quite small and are built of wooden planks with a thatched roof. The floor is beaten clay or earth, and there are long tables and benches for the pupils and a separate table and chair for the teacher. The same subjects are taught as in American or British schools, but learning takes longer because everything is taught in English.

In the larger towns, the schools are built of stone or cement, and many have sports fields. Nigerian schoolchildren are very fond of all forms of games and sport.

After six years at primary school, the best pupils go on to grammar school. As there are not enough grammar schools, there is great competition for places. A school with a hundred places may have as many as a thousand students applying for

Lagos University.

Outside a school building. Organized games are part of the school curriculum in Nigeria.

admission. Most of these schools are boarding schools because the students come from far away.

Nigerians are so eager to learn that they do not always wait for the government or the missionaries to build a school. One of the best schools in Nigeria was started in this way. Some years ago, Tai Solarin—later a famous headmaster—took 70 boys with him to the bush near Ikenne in the Western State. They cleared the forest and built their own school. Five years later, they had built nearly 40 more buildings, and there are now many hundreds of boys and girls attending the school.

Until 1948, a Nigerian student wishing to go to college had to go overseas because there were no universities in Nigeria. But in 1948 the government of the colony of Nigeria founded the country's first university, at Ibadan. The majority of the students train to be teachers, because in a country the size of Nigeria many teachers are needed.

By the time Nigeria became independent in 1960, one university was not sufficient. More and more teachers, doctors, lawyers, and engineers were needed. The first thing the government of independent Nigeria did was to open more universities. Throughout the country, in 1990 there were 35 state and

These young men have been given time off from work to study at this technical training school.

federal universities, polytechnic institutes, and military colleges, plus colleges of education and of agriculture. But the students attending these schools represent less than 1 percent of the 21-29 year olds in Nigeria.

There are many older Nigerians who have never been to school. They are now being given the opportunity of learning to read and write in English. Traveling teachers go around from village to village, and people come from far away to be taught.

Schools and universities have brought Western culture to Nigeria, but the people have had their own learning, art, and culture for a very long time—long before the first Europeans came.

More than 2,000 years ago, in the valley of the Benue River, lived a large tribe named Nok. Although they have disappeared, traces of their civilization can still be seen in the pieces of stone sculpture, pottery, tools, and various implements which they left behind. Then, too, near the Cross River, hidden by the forest, there are monuments of stone, which were left by another tribe. Yoruba artists in Benin and Ife made beautiful objects and statues 600 years ago. The bronze statues of Benin are very famous and so are the figures made of brass.

Where there was no bronze or brass or stone, artists turned to wood. Some trees in Nigeria, such as ebony or ironwood, are extremely hard, and both in the east and west of the country artists carved figures in wood. There are many of these carv-

Musicians with unusual instruments provide music and rhythm for dancers at Kaduna.

ings in the museums of Europe and America and in the new museums of Africa.

In northern Nigeria, where timber is scarce, carving was done in ivory, and craftsmen also worked in silver or gold. The Arab teachers who came to northern Nigeria left behind beautifully written and bound manuscripts. The northern people also built large mosques and made colored tiles for walls and floors.

All Nigerians are fond of music. The music sounds a little strange to European ears because there is no obvious melody. The music is mostly for dancing to, and the main thing about it is the beat or rhythm. Not surprisingly, the chief instrument in Nigerian music is the drum.

Usually, this is made from a hollowed-out log. Across the ends, pieces of fine goatskin are stretched, and between them vertical strands of thin cord are tightly tied, all the way around the drum. By pressing one or more of the cords with his arm, the drummer can produce different sounds. The drum is slung around the shoulder on a strap and is beaten with a short stick.

"Talking" drums are much larger and heavier and are placed on the ground. The ends are not covered and the sounds vary according to the hollowness, thickness, and length of the log. These drums are used for sending messages in country districts where there is no telegraph or telephone.

Dances are part of every entertainment and celebration. Tribes, districts, and villages all have their own traditional dances. Many of them are for men only. Sometimes they com-

A display of dancing, featuring a traditional war dance. The dancers swiftly circle the warrior lying on the ground while the war drum reaches fever pitch.

memorate an event in the past of the tribe. The chief dancer may wear a huge mask and a disguise of feathers and grass. Some costumes are made up entirely of colored beads. The steps vary from dance to dance but they all follow the beat of the drums, the dancers stamping, swaying, and sometimes jumping into the air.

Nigerians enjoy dancing very much. Often a dance will start because somebody has returned home or has passed an examination successfully—or simply for the pleasure of dancing.

12

A Visit to a Small Village

The small villages of Nigeria are not on the main roads. The best way to reach them is by four-wheel drive vehicles. Even so, it is often necessary to walk part of the way. The winding paths in the bush are not made for motor vehicles. Here and there along the path are small clearings where yams or sweet potatoes or banana trees have been planted.

As you approach the village you pass small gardens. The village itself may be completely hidden by the forest until you arrive at the first house.

The houses are quite small and there may be several of them built close together and surrounded by a fence, making what is known as a compound. Some fences consist of spiky plants in a long row. Others are simply stakes driven into the ground and tied together with creepers. As the soil is warm and fertile, many of the stakes begin to sprout and grow leaves, flowers, or even fruit.

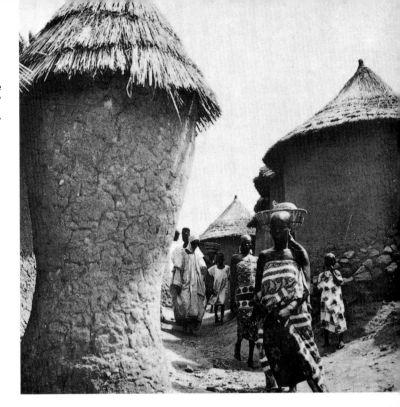

A village "street" scene.

There are no streets in the village, but paths lead from one compound to another.

The houses have no chimneys. Cooking is done inside, and the smoke simply escapes through the thatched roof. In the bigger villages, there is a school, a dispensary where medicines are prepared, and sometimes a postal agency or depot. Once a week the postman comes to the depot to deliver and collect the mail. If the village is Christian, there will also be a small church or chapel.

The villagers keep a wide variety of animals: dogs, hens, ducks, black goats, black pigs, and black sheep.

In the morning, as soon as it is light, everybody in the village is up and about. Girls carrying buckets on their heads can be seen going toward the nearest stream or well to fetch water.

The women begin their washing, or start preparing food. The men go off to their work on the land. Each carries a cutlass or machete. These are heavy knives, about two feet (60 centimeters) in length. They are used for a variety of jobs—to cut through the bush, to dig, to cut firewood, or to chop up meat.

Many of the women go to work in the vegetable gardens. They march off together, carrying their wide-bladed, short-handled hoes on their heads.

All country people go to bed when it becomes dark. For light, they use oil lamps or hurricane lamps, known as "bush lamps." In the larger villages there is a policeman and sometimes a guard for the night, who is known as the "watchnight."

The first thing a visitor does on arrival in a village, is to go and greet the local chief. The headman—or chief—looks and dresses like the other villagers, but he carries a carved or decorated staff.

Visitors are invited into the chief's compound because, like all Nigerians, the headman is pleased to see strangers. He also likes to offer drink and food. The drink may be corn beer made of maize or palm wine from oil-palm trees. The chief usually has his own ceremonial drinking horn and the beer or wine is poured out of a calabash. This is a dried pumpkin with a long, curved neck at one end. Some types of calabash are quite big and are decorated with designs or with beadwork or strips of colored leather.

Inside the house there is very little furniture, but every headman or chief has his stool. It is made from the trunk of a tree and decorated with carvings, representing animals—the leopard is a common choice—or human figures. The visitors are offered a simple chair or stool to sit on. But nobody sits down or speaks unless he is first invited to by his host.

The village chief is a very important man in Nigeria. He knows everybody and he is the link between the government and the people.

When he has to make a major decision, he asks his friends in the village to come and talk the matter over with him. The village may need a new school, or the people may want a better road. The matter is discussed by the village council. Sometimes, the council will meet in the open, with everyone sitting under a big, shady tree. When the question has been settled, the chief goes to a government official in the nearest big town and speaks for his people.

Villagers like to form themselves into clubs or societies. Men and women of more or less the same age form groups to help one another. If one member has a son who is a promising student, his club or society will lend him money to pay for further studies. The money will be repaid to the society once the student starts earning.

Most villagers earn their living by farming. If the village is a long way from the main road, the men take their produce to the nearest big village where there is a market. In the market their produce is bought by a trader who transports it to the towns. Sometimes the farmers do not sell their goods for money, but exchange them for something they need. This is called "barter-trade."

Until the European traders came, the Nigerians did not buy and sell things for money. In the southern part of Nigeria,

Factory skills are being learned by the people of Nigeria. This picture shows the production of polythene bags.

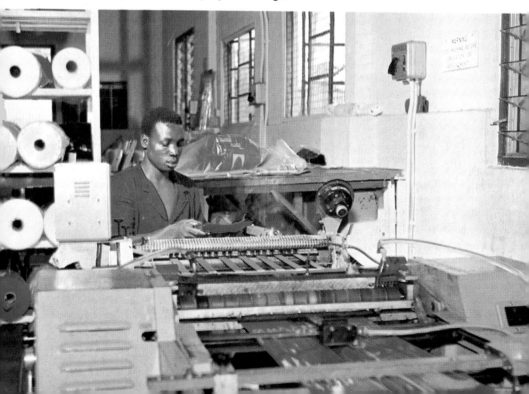

cowrie shells were used as money. In the north, the cattle-owning tribes counted their wealth in cattle: the more cattle a man owned, the richer he was. Gold and silver were recognized as valuable, but were not used for money, and paper money was unsuitable because the people could not read and could not therefore understand what the different banknotes signified. There are remote places in Nigeria where even now the people do not like paper money and prefer to use coins.

Many young men leave the villages to work on plantations or in factories in the towns, where they can make more money. Although they often visit their homes, once they have lived in a large town many of them do not wish to return to live in their villages any more.

13

Nigeria's Place in Africa

When, in 1960, independence came to Nigeria, the Queen of England became the queen of independent Nigeria. But many Nigerians felt that it was not right for a strange ruler, living far away, to be the head of their country. So they decided to turn Nigeria into a republic and to have a president of their own. But, at the same time, they chose to remain a member of the British Commonwealth.

Because the British governed the country for so many years, they had much influence on the way the country is run. The police force, for example, follows the British pattern, and the legal system is based on that of England.

Nevertheless, some laws which work well in Britain do not always work in Nigeria. And there are also many tribal laws and customs which the people have followed for centuries and which are important to them. So the country has two separate kinds of law which work side by side; there are the laws made by the government of Nigeria and those of the tribes.

After its independence, Nigeria became a very good example to other African countries in its improvements in education and healthcare. It learned from the Europeans and used this knowledge intelligently. More children go to school in Nigeria than in any other African country. Then, too, it also has learned how to overcome many of the tropical diseases; and, where diseases such as leprosy do still occur, the government—that is, the whole country—cares for the sick people.

Other African countries have sent their people to Nigeria to see how it manages its affairs, and Nigeria sends its teachers and professors to advise other countries on how to run their schools and universities. In addition, many lawyers, architects, doctors, nurses, and engineers have been sent by Nigeria to other African countries.

In 1963, Nigeria decided to become part of the Organization of African States. The countries belonging to this organization work to create a better life for all Africans.

In a country as huge as Nigeria, where so many millions of people live, it takes time to improve the general standard of living. Nigeria has been independent for a very few years, and its way of life is changing all the time. There is not enough money to pay for all the improvements which are needed, so Nigeria has to rely on help from other countries.

Much of this help is given by the United Nations, which is an association of all the countries of the world. This association has established special groups giving technical aid. One group helps farmers to grow better crops and to breed healthier animals.

Nigeria is a member of
the World Health
Organization. The
group is conscious of
the need for facilities
like those shown here
in a modern hospital.

Another group advises on education and improved living conditions. Then there is the World Health Organization, which tries to ensure that the people lead healthier lives. Nigeria itself is a member of these groups and it, in its turn, helps other countries as much as it can.

Aid comes from other directions as well. There are teachers from the United States and Britain; missionaries from Ireland; there are Dutch farming experts and many others.

One hundred years ago, Nigeria was an enormous stretch of land inhabited by many different tribes who were kept in order by a foreign government. Today it is an independent country working hard toward the betterment of all the tribes that make up its citizens.

Unfortunately, in the 1960s the bitter strife between the federal government of Nigeria and the breakaway state of Biafra delayed the country's security and progress. Those threats were successfully overcome, but others followed. Nigeria's quest to gain civilian rule after years of military regimes continues and the future remains uncertain. However, there can be no doubt that Nigeria has secured for herself a well-deserved position among the countries of modern Africa.

The Supreme Court Lagos—one example of Nigeria's efforts to establish the rule of a just law at the time of independence.

GLOSSARY

artesian wells   Very deep wells bored into the dry soil of the desert areas to reach water

barter-trade   Exchanging items you produce for items you need instead of for money

emir   Ruler or chief in Islamic countries

foo-foo   Dough made from ground maize (corn)

garri   Food made from the roots of the cassava plant

groundnuts   What Americans call peanuts; thousands of tons of them are grown each year in Nigeria

harmattan   Desert wind that blows into Nigeria from the Sahara making the air foggy with dust; the wind can last for two months

latex   White liquid from the rubber tree that is used to make rubber

lorry   Motor truck

machete   Heavy knife about two feet in length, used for a variety of jobs including cutting through shrubs and bushes, digging, cutting firewood, and chopping meat

oba   King

oja   Long, wide piece of cloth women wear around their waists

savannah   Grassland with few trees and some small shrubs

INDEX

Vultures, 42

W
Water, discovery of, 78-79
Waterways, 65
Western Region, 18, 20
Wildlife, 41-42
Witch doctors, 58

Y
Yams, 67
Yola, 65
Yorubas, 16, 18, 20, 22, 23, 27, 28-30, 53, 84

Z
"Zik." *See* Azikiwe, Nnamdi